At the Zoo

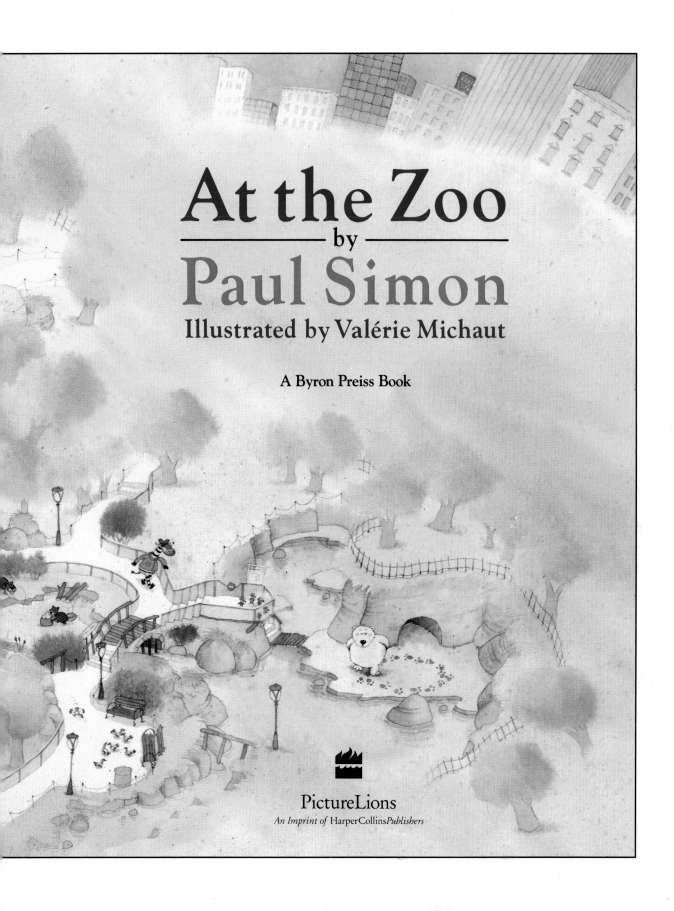

At the Zoo
by
Paul Simon
Illustrated by Valérie Michaut

A Byron Preiss Book

PictureLions

An Imprint of HarperCollinsPublishers

Someone told me
it's all happening
at the zoo.
I do believe it,
I do believe it's true.

It's a light and tumble journey
from the East Side to the park.

Just a fine and fancy ramble to the zoo.

But you can take the crosstown bus
if it's raining or it's cold.

And the animals will love it if you do.

Something tells me
it's all happening
at the zoo.
I do believe it,
I do believe it's true.

POLAR BEAR ➔

GiRAFFE ➔

NT ➔

POLAR BEA

The monkeys stand for honesty.

Giraffes are insincere.

And the elephants are kindly but they're dumb.

Orangutans are sceptical
of changes in their cages.

And the zookeeper is very fond of Rum.

Zebras are reactionaries.

Antelopes are missionaries.

Pigeons plot in secrecy…

...and hamsters turn on frequently.

What a gas!

You gotta come
and see at the zoo!

Paul Simon began his career as the songwriter
with the award-winning duo, Simon and Garfunkel.
Since going solo in 1970, Mr Simon's recording success
has continued, most noteably with his 1986 album
"Graceland", which won two Grammy Awards.

Valérie Michaut, illustrator of the 1990 UNICEF
calendar, is one of France's leading young children's
book illustrators.

First published in the USA by Doubleday, a division of
Bantam Doubleday Dell Publishing Group, Inc, 1991
Published in HarperCollins 1991
First published in Picture Lions 1992

Picture Lions is an imprint of the Children's Division,
part of HarperCollins Publishers Limited,
77-85 Fulham Palace Road, Hammersmith,
London W6 8JB

Special thanks to Stephen Rubin, Shaye Areheart,
Jacqueline Onassis, Peter Kruzan, Stephen and
Nathalie Brenninkmeyer, Marino Degano,
and the Central Park Zoo

Editor: Gillian Bucky

Printed in Hong Kong